# Chemtastrophe!

# Body Care Chemistry

Rachel Eagen

Crabtree Publishing Company
www.crabtreebooks.com

# Crabtree Publishing Company
## www.crabtreebooks.com

**Publishing plan research and development:**

Sean Charlebois, Reagan Miller
Crabtree Publishing Company

**Developed and Produced by:** Plan B Book Packagers

**Editorial director:** Ellen Rodger

**Art director:** Rosie Gowsell-Pattison

**Glossary and index:** Nina Butz

**Project coordinator:** Kathy Middleton

**Editor:** Adrianna Morganelli

**Proofreader:** Molly Aloian

**Prepress technician and production coordinator:**

Margaret Amy Salter

**Print coordinator:** Katherine Berti

**Special thanks to experimenter Gillian**

**Photographs:** Title page: Laurence Gough/Shutterstock Inc.; p.2 : Wikimedia Commons; p. 3: Teacept/Shutterstock Inc.; p. 4: (top) R. Gino Santa Maria/Shutterstock Inc., (bottom) Laurence Gough/Shutterstock Inc.; p. 5: (bottom) Granite/ Shutterstock Inc., (top) Lev Olkha/Shutterstock Inc.; p. 6: Apollofoto/ Shutterstock Inc.; p. 7: (top) Bike Rider London/ Shutterstock Inc., (bottom) Tatiana Popova/Shutterstock Inc.; p. 8: (top) Urfin/Shutterstock Inc., (bottom) S.M./ Shutterstock Inc.; p. 9: (top) Mike Ledray/Shutterstock Inc., (bottom) Optimarc/ Shutterstock Inc.; p. 10: Sparkling Moments Photography/ Shutterstock Inc.; p. 11: Emin Kuliyev/Shutterstock Inc.; p. 12: Denisk/Shutterstock Inc.; p. 13: (top) Kynata/ Shutterstock Inc., (bottom) Ruzanna/Shutterstock Inc.; p. 14: iofoto/Shutterstock Inc.; p. 15: (top) Stephen Gibson/Shutterstock Inc., (bottom) Skazka Grez/Shutterstock Inc.; p. 16: (top) Nikita Chisnikov/ Shutterstock Inc., (bottom) Wikimedia Commons; p. 17: (left) OSTILL/ iStockPhoto.com, (right) Ra3rn/Shutterstock Inc.; p. 18-19: Laurence Gough/Shutterstock Inc.; p. 20-23: Jim Chernishenko/ Shutterstock Inc.; p. 24: (right) Diane39/ iStockPhoto.com; (left) Jeka/Shutterstock Inc.; p. 25: (top) Ipatov/Shutterstock Inc. (bottom); p. 26: (bottom) Dan Thomas Brostrom/Shutterstock Inc., (top) Tyler Olson/ Shutterstock Inc.; p. 27: (bottom) Capture Light/ Shutterstock Inc., (top) Phil Date/Shutterstock Inc.; p. 28: Denisk/Shutterstock Inc.; p. 29: (top) Laurence Gough/ Shutterstock Inc. (bottom) Wikimedia Commons; p. 30-31: Teacept/Shutterstock Inc.

 "How we know" boxes feature an image of 18th century French scientist Antoine Lavoisier who conducted some of the first quantitative chemical experiments. He was also the first to identify the components of water and air, and he helped develop the metric system which helped standardize measurement in scientific testing. His work earned him the title "father of modern chemistry."

**Library and Archives Canada Cataloguing in Publication**

Eagen, Rachel, 1979-
    Body care chemistry / Rachel Eagen.

(Chemtastrophe!)
Includes index.
Issued also in electronic format.
ISBN 978-0-7787-5282-0 (bound).--ISBN 978-0-7787-5288-2 (pbk.)

    1. Cosmetics--Analysis--Juvenile literature. 2. Health products--Analysis--Juvenile literature. 3. Chemistry--Experiments--Juvenile literature. I. Title.
II. Series: Chemtastrophe!

TP983.E23 2011          j668'.5          C2010-906574-3

**Library of Congress Cataloging-in-Publication Data**

Eagen, Rachel, 1979-
  Body care chemistry / Rachel Eagen.
      p. cm. -- (Chemtastrophe!)
  Includes index.
  ISBN 978-0-7787-5288-2 (pbk. : alk. paper) -- ISBN 978-0-7787-5282-0 (reinforced library binding : alk. paper) -- ISBN 978-1-4271-9607-1 (electronic pdf.)
  1. Cosmetics--Materials--Juvenile literature. 2. Heath products--Materials--Juvenile literature. 3. Chemistry--Experiments--Juvenile literature. I. Title.
II. Series.

TP983.E24 2011
668'.5--dc22

                                        2010042060

# Crabtree Publishing Company

www.crabtreebooks.com          1-800-387-7650

Printed in China/012011/GW20101014

**Published in Canada**
**Crabtree Publishing**
616 Welland Ave.
St. Catharines, ON
L2M 5V6

**Published in the United States**
**Crabtree Publishing**
PMB 59051
350 Fifth Avenue, 59th Floor
New York, New York 10118

**Published in the United Kingdom**
**Crabtree Publishing**
Maritime House
Basin Road North, Hove
BN41 1WR

**Published in Australia**
**Crabtree Publishing**
386 Mt. Alexander Rd.
Ascot Vale (Melbourne)
VIC 3032

# Contents

# Lucky Accidents

Have you ever looked at something—a leaf or a glass full of water—and wanted to know more about it? How does a leaf grow? What makes water stay in the glass rather than spill all over the floor? The answers to these questions are rooted in science. In fact, simply asking them is a big part of what scientists do every day.

## Science is Knowledge

The word science comes from a Latin word, *scientia*, which means knowledge. Science is about looking at the world with open eyes, asking questions, and seeking to answer those questions through research and experimentation. Research is a process of gathering information, while experimentation involves testing ideas and drawing up **theories**. Science is a huge field. It covers many different areas of research in medicine, technology, mathematics, and computer science. Scientists live in every part of the world, and they are constantly coming up with new ideas that further our understanding of the world in which we live.

What makes water stay in a glass? These are the types of questions scientists ask and seek answers to.

4

# The First Scientists

Humans have always been curious about their surroundings. This curiosity has led to many discoveries. In a way, these discoveries can be thought of as lucky accidents, because it is hard to predict what will happen when you try something for the first time. One of the first accidental discoveries happened when humans learned how to make and use fire. Learning to use fire is probably the most important development in human history, partly because it led to many discoveries in a special field of scientific study called chemistry.

# The Science of Chemistry

Chemistry is the study of matter, which makes up everything you can see, as well as everything you cannot see. The study of chemistry is also about creating and observing chemical reactions, in which two or more things react, or work together, to create something new. Chemists study the properties, or nature of things, in the world around us, as well as special **substances** that are created in laboratories. Chemistry is a big part of our lives. It is thanks to chemistry that we have medicines to treat illness, fuel to power vehicles, clothes to wear, and food to eat. It is also thanks to chemistry that we have products to look after our bodies, including soap, toothpaste, and shampoo.

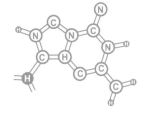

All natural products, such as some toothpastes or soaps, require the skills of a chemist to make them and to ensure the mixtures and solutions are safe.

# Heart of the Matter

**Everything is made up of matter. The paper and ink used to make this book, the chair you might be sitting on, the food you eat, and the sheets you sleep in every night are matter. Your entire body is also made of matter—your skin, hair, fingernails, and bones.**

## Matter is Everywhere

Matter is made up of tiny **particles** that you cannot see. That probably seems strange, since you can see your body and the book in front of you. The particles are so tiny that it takes a very powerful microscope to see them. These particles hold onto each other, forming a blob of material that we can see on our own—your shirt, your hands, your school desk. These particles are called atoms.

## All About Atoms

Atoms have three parts: protons, neutrons, and electrons. The protons and neutrons bind together at the core of the atom, forming the **nucleus**. When two or more atoms cling together, it is called a molecule. The atoms are attracted to each other like magnets. Thousands of molecules need to line up together to form something that you can see, even something very small, such as a single eyelash.

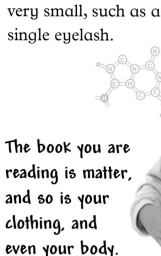

The book you are reading is matter, and so is your clothing, and even your body.

# Matter on the Move

When scientists talk about matter, they talk about three different states of matter: solid, liquid, and gas. All matter is in one of these states at all times. In each of these states, the atoms that make up matter move, but the movement is impossible to see. The atoms move differently depending on what state (solid, liquid, gas) that they are in. In a solid, the atoms move very little. They are packed together very tightly, allowing the solid to keep its shape. A stick of deodorant, a cake of makeup, and a bar of soap are all examples of solids.

# Liquid and Gas

The atoms of a liquid are spaced further apart. That is why liquids can flow and be poured. They can also pool into puddles, be slurped through a straw, and course down a stream. Liquids do not have a definite shape. They take the shape of the container that holds them. Hair spray, perfume, and shampoo are examples of liquids. The atoms of a gas are spaced furthest apart. Gases take up as much as they possibly can. Imagine a thin trail of smoke escaping from a chimney. The smoke rises into the sky and spreads out, eventually taking so much space that you can no longer see it. Canned air freshener and steam from a hot shower are examples of gases.

A milkshake is a liquid and fries and burgers are solids...but they are all matter!

Hair spray is a liquid state of matter.

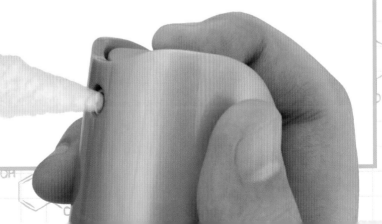

# Changes of State

States of matter do not always stay the same. Changes of state occur as molecules gain or lose energy. One way to give matter energy is to heat it up. Think of what would happen if you placed an ice cube in a frying pan. As a solid ice cube, water molecules have very little energy, allowing the cube to keep its shape. In the warm air, the water molecules gain energy and start moving further apart, eventually melting into a liquid, becoming a wet pool in the bottom of the pan. If you turned on the burner, the water molecules would gain even more energy, turning into a gas and rising into the air as steam. In chemistry, a change of state is described as a physical change. That is because the water is still water in all of its different states. The steam may **condense** on the ceiling, becoming a liquid again, and if you collected the water droplets in a glass and returned them to the freezer, the water would freeze into ice once again.

Ice cubes change state from liquid to solid when they freeze, and back to liquid when they melt.

# fun fact

**Adding pollutants, such as toxic chemicals, to water decreases its surface tension.**

# Elements and Compounds

All atoms are not the same. In fact, scientists have identified over 100 different kinds of atoms. They differ depending on how many protons they have in their nucleus. Every different kind of atom is called an element, and all of the known atoms belong to a chart known as the periodic table of elements. This table is very important to chemists around the world. In the table, the elements are listed according to how many protons they have. For example, the first element is called hydrogen. It has a single proton, and for this reason, it has the atomic number 1. When two or more different kinds of atoms, or elements combine, they create a new substance called a compound molecule, which chemists simply call compounds. A water molecule, for example, is a compound made up of two hydrogen atoms and one oxygen atom.

Chemists deal with mixtures and compounds.

A water strider insect demonstrates surface tension.

## Surface Tension

Take a pitcher of water and fill a drinking glass. Fill it all the way to the top, to the point where it almost spills over the sides of the glass. Now look closely at the water. What do you notice? If you have filled the glass completely full, you will see that the water seems to rise above the rim of the glass. You will also notice that the top of the water looks like it is covered with a thin skin-like layer. In liquids, like molecules, or molecules that are the same, cling together as closely as they can. On the surface of the water, some of the water molecules touch air molecules, which makes them want to cling even closer together. This effect is called surface tension.

# Method and Means

Scientists work hard to develop ideas about the way the world works. They learn all that they can by reading, testing, and analyzing information. They then create new knowledge, either by building on a discovery made by another scientist, or by proving that a previously accepted idea is wrong.

## Making Predictions

A big part of being a scientist is making predictions. A prediction is sort of like a guess, but scientists usually make what are called educated guesses. That means that their guesses are based on things they already know to be true. Predictions are the basis for a lot of scientific research. Scientists can build experiments based on information they hope to prove to be true. Sometimes, these experiments prove scientists very wrong, but that is okay because some of the greatest scientific discoveries have happened when scientists were proven wrong.

Science requires good observation skills.

10

## fun fact

"I am not accustomed to saying anything with certainty after only one or two observations."
–Andreas Vesalius, Belgian scientist (1514-1564)

# Testing

Scientists conduct experiments in order to test their ideas. In an experiment, a scientist **simulates** an event under controlled conditions. In other words, the scientist works hard to make sure that the experiment happens in conditions that do not change, such as in a lab, using the same tools, making accurate, consistent measurements. Controlled conditions are important for producing similar results experiment after experiment. Scientists usually have to prove their findings several times, which means doing the experiment over and over again—sometimes hundreds of times!

# Theories and Laws

Once scientists have tested an idea over and over under controlled conditions, they draw up scientific theories that explain their findings. Theories explain things that happen repeatedly in nature. They often require many years of research. These theories may be shortened into scientific laws, which are simple statements of scientific truths.

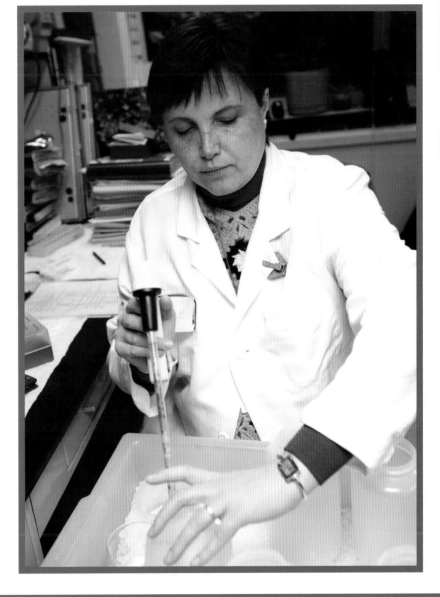

Experiments are a part of life for scientists, so they follow a set of rules that allow them to trust the results of their experiments.

# Day-to-day Chemistry

You now know how much time and effort are behind scientific theories, laws, and ideas. But it is not just theories and ideas that are tested in science labs. The products we use on our bodies every day, the foods we eat, and the chemicals used on our lawns and gardens are all developed and tested in labs, too.

## Look Around You

The next time you are in a drug store, take a look at the products on the shelves. Every item in the store is a product of chemistry, from the drugs behind the prescription counter, to the shampoo and bath products and household cleaners, to the perfumes and makeup in the cosmetics department. Take a look at the label of any of these products. You will see a list of words that are hard to pronounce—these are chemicals. Even the plastic and glass containers used to package all of these products come from chemistry labs.

Antoine Lavoisier (1743-1793) was a wealthy French nobleman known today as the father of modern chemistry because of his experiments.

# fun fact

The first chemistry textbook was published in 1789. The book was written by French chemist Antoine Lavoisier, and was called *Traité Élémentaire de Chimie*.

# Making New Products

The products we use go through years of testing before they are made available to consumers. It is not as simple of a process as you might think. Chemists who work for cosmetics companies are constantly inventing and testing new products for different purposes. Sometimes, these products are designed for convenience. Two-in-one shampoo, for example, was designed to be convenient. The idea behind it was that consumers could buy one product rather than two—both shampoo and conditioner. How was the product made? It was not as easy as mixing shampoo and conditioner together in one bottle. A special product had to be formulated by chemists, so it would lather like a shampoo, but soften and detangle hair like a conditioner.

Many body care products, such as shampoos, are specially formulated in chemistry labs for specific hair types or uses.

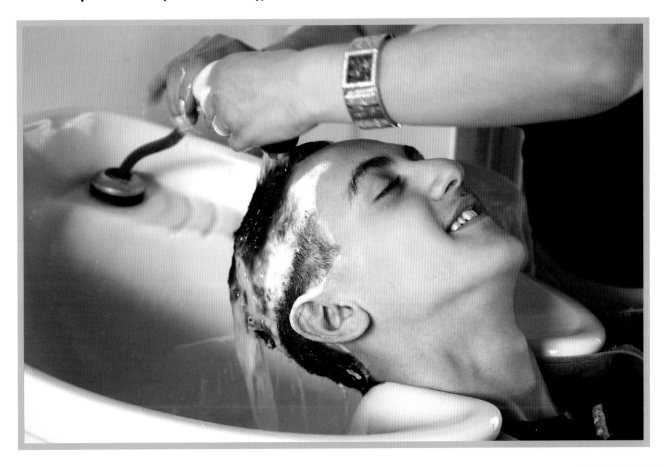

# Bathroom Chemistry

Every day, you put several different products on your body. They all come from chemistry labs, even the products that are labeled "organic" or "natural." But what is in these products and how do they work?

## Lather Up!

Shampoo is a liquid **detergent** that is used to clean hair. In the world of chemistry, shampoo is known as a solution, which means it is a homogeneous mixture. Homogeneous means that it looks the same throughout—there are no floating bits or oily layers that stay unmixed. You do not have to shake a bottle of shampoo before you use it, unlike salad dressing. In the past, shampoo was made by boiling animal fats in water with herbs to make it smell nice. Today, shampoo has a special substance known to chemists as a **surfactant**.

Dog shampoo is different than human shampoo because it contains less of a chemical called sulphate. Dogs need more oil for their coats to prevent itching.

# Surfactants

The expression oil and water don't mix rings true when it comes to body care. Every minute, our skin secretes an oil, sebum, to help moisturize our skin. We need sebum to keep from shriveling up, but too much sebum can lead to dandruff, pimples, and other skin problems. Sebum also has an odor, and traps dirt and pollutants from the air, covering us in a fine film of filth. That is why we wash our skin and hair regularly. Water cannot do the job on its own because it beads up when it comes in contact with all of that oil on our bodies. That is where surfactants come in.

Surfactants are chemicals that lower the surface tension of water. Surface tension is the tendency of liquids to cling together, especially in the presence of a gas or solid, such as sebum. Surfactants lower the surface tension of liquids so they can mix with solids. In other words, surfactants in shampoo allow the soapy water to penetrate the oils in your hair, leaving it clean and smelling nice.

Too much sebum
can cause pimples.

15

# The Dope on Soap

Soap works in the same way as shampoo. It is traditionally sold in solid bars, but liquid body washes do the same job and are used for the same purpose as bar soaps. Like shampoo, soap has surfactants that help to dissolve oil and dirt on the skin. Two other important ingredients that are used to make soap are fatty acids and a **base**, such as lye. Fatty acids come from vegetable oils or animal fats. Lye is a strong chemical that can burn the skin if it is not mixed with other substances. It has been used in soap-making for centuries. When soap molecules come in contact with skin, they work to lift away sebum and dirt. To understand more about acids and bases, it will help to know something about pH.

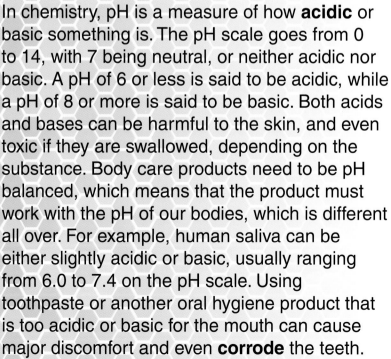

Surfactants dissolve oil through a chemical reaction.

# HOW WE KNOW

## What is pH?

In chemistry, pH is a measure of how **acidic** or basic something is. The pH scale goes from 0 to 14, with 7 being neutral, or neither acidic nor basic. A pH of 6 or less is said to be acidic, while a pH of 8 or more is said to be basic. Both acids and bases can be harmful to the skin, and even toxic if they are swallowed, depending on the substance. Body care products need to be pH balanced, which means that the product must work with the pH of our bodies, which is different all over. For example, human saliva can be either slightly acidic or basic, usually ranging from 6.0 to 7.4 on the pH scale. Using toothpaste or another oral hygiene product that is too acidic or basic for the mouth can cause major discomfort and even **corrode** the teeth.

# Battling Body Odor

Deodorant is a product that people apply to their armpits to fight body odor, or B.O. A common misunderstanding about sweat is that it smells bad. The truth is that most sweat smells like nothing at all, at first. The stink comes from **bacteria** that live on our skin (yes, even after you wash). Bacteria love warm, wet places, so our armpits become a playground for bacteria to eat, poop, and breed—P-U!

What most people do not know is that the skin in the armpits is naturally acidic, having a pH of 4.5 to 6. When you wash, you destroy the acidity of your skin, making it neutral or basic. This actually encourages bacteria to grow, as they thrive in highly basic or acidic environments. This is how deodorants can help. Most deodorants contain alcohol, a substance known to kill bacteria, or prevent them from multiplying in the first place. Antiperspirants work even harder to minimize body odor by preventing you from sweating. Chemicals by the names of aluminum chloride, aluminum chlorohydrate, and aluminum zirconium are used in antiperspirants because they block sweat ducts in the skin.

Body odor is a chemical reaction in our bodies!

# Let's Test That

**If you want to be a chemist, you need to learn how to experiment. All scientific experiments are broken down into six basic steps, which help to organize the work in a way that is easy for others to understand.**

## State Your Purpose

The purpose is your reason for doing the experiment. What do you want to know? What are you hoping to find out? Your purpose could be simple or complicated. Your purpose should be very specific and involve a single question or statement. After designing a question, you must do your research and gather information to find an answer. Research helps you prepare for the experiment. Sometimes, research gives you a better idea of how the experiment might turn out.

## The Hypothesis

A hypothesis is an educated guess, or prediction, about what will happen during the experiment. A hypothesis is a statement. Sometimes, the statement differs from the findings. Try not to worry about your experiment turning out differently from your hypothesis—being surprised is a big part of being a scientist!

Determining a hypothesis requires some investigation and research.

# Experiment

This is where you explain what you are going to do. Break the experiment down into small steps that are easy to follow.

It may take time to observe what is happening in an experiment.

# Make Observations

In this section, you explain everything that you observe, during the experiment. It helps to take notes during the experiment so you will not forget to include anything in your write-up later. Sometimes, this section is called Analysis.

# Conclusions and Analysis

What happened? Were you surprised? Was your hypothesis correct? In this section, you explain what you discovered during the experiment. It is okay if your hypothesis was "wrong," just be sure to record your results honestly. Remember, experimentation is all about learning and having fun.

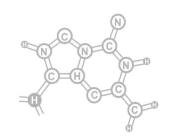

# Toothpick Tornado

**Have you ever thought about how shampoo cleans your hair?**

Question:
How quickly does shampoo change the surface tension of water?

Hypothesis:
Adding a drop of shampoo to a bowl of water should rapidly decrease its surface tension.

## Materials:

wooden toothpicks
dropper or spoon
bowl
water
shampoo

## Method:

1. Fill a large bowl halfway with water.
2. Place a small dab of shampoo on the blunt, fat end of a toothpick.
3. Place the toothpick in the water. Record your observations.

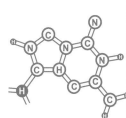

When the bowl is filled, add a drop or dab of shampoo to the toothpick end.

Gently place the toothpick into the water, watch how long it takes to move to the side.

Record your observations.

## Results and Discussion:

When the toothpick was placed in the water, it moved forward (pointed end first). How long did this take?

The shampoo on the blunt end of the toothpick lowered the surface tension of the water, propelling the pointed end of the toothpick across the water where the surface tension was stronger. This shows that the surfactants in shampoo quickly lower the surface tension of water, making shampoo an excellent product for cleaning hair.

# Acid or Base?

In this experiment you will make your own formula for testing pH, and then use it to test the body care products you use every day.

**Question:** What is the pH of various body care products?

**Hypothesis:** Body care products have different pH levels to work on different parts of the body.

## Materials:

¼ cup (60 ml) of white vinegar
½ teaspoon (2 grams) tumeric (a spice)
1 teaspoon (4 grams) baking soda
¼ cup (60 ml) water
½ cup (120 ml) rubbing alcohol
bowl and a clear glass
cotton swabs

## Procedure:

1. Mix the tumeric and the rubbing alcohol in a bowl.
2. Mix the water and baking soda in the glass.
3. Pour a bit of the tumeric mixture into the glass. Observe and record.
3. Slowly pour the vinegar into the drinking glass. Observe and record.

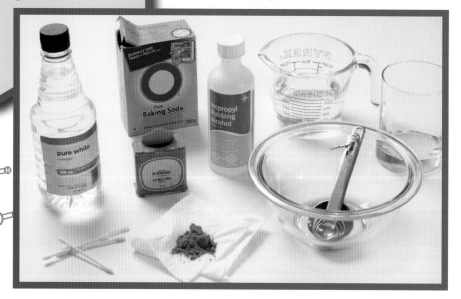

What color does the mixture turn?

What happens when you add the vinegar?

Soak one end of about ten cotton swabs in the tumeric-alcohol mixture for about three to five minutes. Let the swabs dry on a plate and when dry use the swabs to test the pH of soap and other body care products.

## Results and Discussion:

A pH indicator changes color to indicate acidic or basic solutions. In acidic solutions, the tumeric indicator stays yellow. In basic solutions, it turns red. Baking soda is basic and turns the mixture red. Vinegar is an acid and turns back to yellow. The vinegar also reacts with the baking soda, neutralizing it and making it bubble.

How acidic or basic are your body care products?

# Eureka! Amazing!

**Scientists at toil in their labs, intent on finding the answer to one question, often stumble upon an answer to a very different question. The history of chemistry and body care show us many examples of this.**

## Soap That Floats

In the late 1800s, William Procter and James Gamble began making their fortune selling their soaps and candles in Cincinnati. But the two businessmen hit the big time when one of their factory workers accidentally invented Ivory, more famously known as "the soap that floats." According to legend, one of the workers left a machine running when he left for lunch, allowing extra air to be pumped into the soap mixture. Once the soap had hardened, workers at Procter and Gamble were amazed to find that it floated! Bars were cut and sent to consumers, who loved the floating soap.

## Bald no more!

Minoxidil is a drug that was developed to treat **high blood pressure**. What patients soon discovered was the drug's interesting side effect: it helped grow hair! Balding patients were thrilled. A topical formula was later developed and marketed under the brand name Rogaine. The secret behind minoxidil is that it is a vasodilator, which means that it increases blood circulation. When applied to the scalp, blood vessels in the hair follicles widen, allowing blood and nutrients to circulate in the **follicle**. This encourages hair growth.

Some discoveries, such as floating soap and treatments for baldness, were unintentional.

# Making It Up

People have been wearing cosmetics for thousands of years, mixing various plants and minerals to create eyeliner and lip color. The term "makeup" actually came into use in the early 1900s, with the success of a specially formulated lightweight greasepaint made for actors by **cosmetician** Max Factor. Factor worked in Hollywood, selling and applying heavy theater greasepaint sticks to film actors' faces. The paint would often crack and melt during shoots, so it had to be reapplied frequently. Frustrated with this, Factor thought like a chemist and experimented with ingredients, inventing the first lightweight makeup that did not crack. He sold it in squeezable tubes in many different skin tone shades. Factor's family company later created pancake makeup, a solid cake makeup originally for the film industry, which later became the biggest and most popular makeup seller.

Max Factor used his knowledge of chemistry and the film industry to create a better makeup.

# HOW WE KNOW

## The Science of Hair Coloring

Do you know that hairdressers are chemists of a sort? They are doing basic chemistry when they color, chemically straighten, or otherwise "do" your hair. The first **synthetic** hair color products were invented in 1909, by French chemist Eugene Schuller. Hairdressers have acted as salon chemists ever since. Hair dye is a mixture of chemicals, but most contain hydrogen peroxide or ammonia. Hydrogen peroxide is a chemical that helps to lift the natural pigment in hair, readying it for the artificial color to go on top. Ammonia also helps to bleach the natural color out of hair, and helps the artificial dye to fasten to each strand of hair.

# Chemistry of Hair

Some people are born with curly hair and some people are born with straight hair. Chemistry makes it possible to change our hair texture. Like many things in your body, hair is made of protein. Within your hair's protein molecules are sulfur atoms called sulfides. The atoms come together to form something called a disulfide bond. If the sulfur atoms in the same protein are not close together but join to form a bond, the protein will bend and create curl. The more disulfide bonds, the curlier the hair. To straighten or relax hair, the bonds must be broken chemically. To make hair curly, disulfide bonds must be chemically forced or created. Hairdressers call this a permanent wave, or perm, but it isn't permanent because new hair grows in straight.

Straightening hair requires a chemical process.

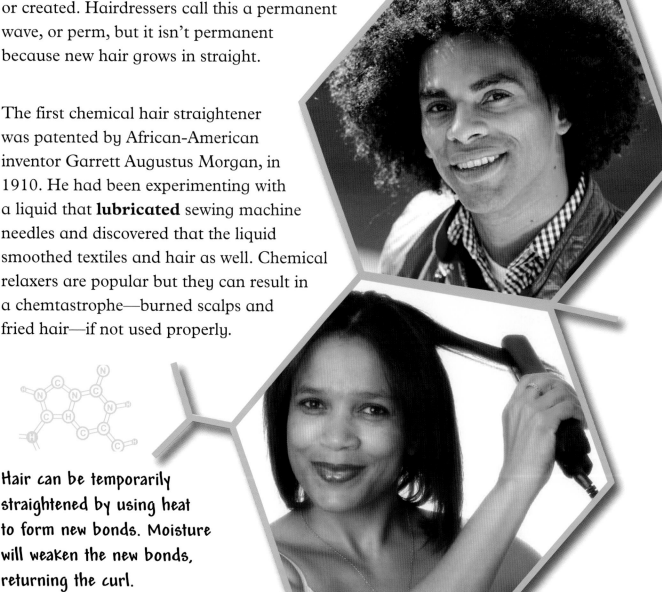

The first chemical hair straightener was patented by African-American inventor Garrett Augustus Morgan, in 1910. He had been experimenting with a liquid that **lubricated** sewing machine needles and discovered that the liquid smoothed textiles and hair as well. Chemical relaxers are popular but they can result in a chemtastrophe—burned scalps and fried hair—if not used properly.

Hair can be temporarily straightened by using heat to form new bonds. Moisture will weaken the new bonds, returning the curl.

# Skin Care 101

Cosmetics companies employ small armies of chemists to develop new products and improve old ones. They create everything from cleansers and skin creams to perfumes and makeup. They use ingredients that are thousands of years old, as well as new materials and compounds. Most skin creams are emulsions, which is a chemistry term for a **dispersion** of one liquid into another. They are often use with emollients, which are fats that soften the skin. Chemists have to know how different ingredients will react with each other, so that the products will be safe to create and safe to use. In the United States, the Federal Food, Drug, and Cosmetic Act was passed in 1938, requiring manufacturers to show that a product was safe before it was sold to the public.

Lavender is known for its relaxing fragrance. Lavender's scent and properties are extracted by chemists and used to scent soaps, creams, and perfumes.

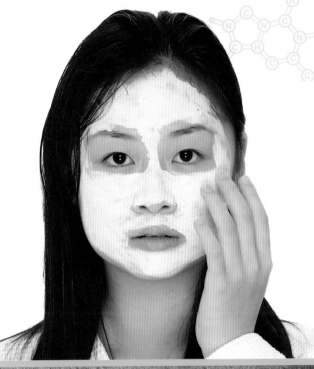

Skin creams were created through trial and error.

# fun fact

Chemists can write the composition of fragrances in their own "language" of chemical structure. That means they can "see" what a scent (or odor) looks like.

# Creative Chemists

**Over time, important chemists have altered our understanding of the world, which has led to huge advancements in medicine, technology, and other fields.**

## Chemistry in Our World

Chemistry plays a huge role in the world today. It is hard to believe that just a few hundred years ago, chemistry was not even recognized as a real science. There are now dozens of different fields of chemistry, which means that chemists usually specialize. For example, biochemistry is the study of chemicals and chemical reactions in living things (humans, plants, and animals). Neurochemistry is the study of brain chemicals that control the way people feel and behave. Other types of chemistry, such as chemical engineering, have applications in the development of fuel and explosives.

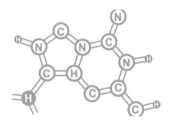

Dutch chemist Jacobus Henricus Van't Hoff won the first ever Nobel Prize for Chemistry in 1901.

## Early Chemists

Greek philosopher Democritus (c. 460-370 BC) was the first person to suggest that matter is made up of tiny particles that we cannot see. He named these particles atoms. This was the beginning of what chemists call atomic theory. In 1800, British scientist John Dalton contributed some new ideas about atoms. Dalton's atomic theory revolutionized chemistry, because it helped other scientists to better understand the way atoms behave. It also gave scientists a better idea of what happens during a chemical reaction.

# Chemist Life

So, just where do chemists work, and what do they do all day? Depending on the kind of work involved, chemists may work in labs, developing or testing new products such as perfumes, food, medicines, fuels, or agricultural **fertilizers**. Other chemists do not create products, and they do not spend any time in labs. Still others conduct environmental research, coming up with new ways to clean up oil spills and other disasters.

Chemists spend years in school studying science.

# HOW WE KNOW

## From Alchemy to Chemistry

In 1661, British inventor, chemist, and philosopher Robert Boyle published *The Sceptical Chymist*, a book that qualified chemistry as a true scientific field. Until this time, chemistry was associated with **alchemy,** which is not a true science. Alchemists were known for their attempts to create gold from common metals. In *The Sceptical Chymist*, Boyle outlined some important ideas about atoms, molecules, and chemical reactions. Many believe this work marked the beginning of modern chemistry. Boyle soon went on to develop Boyle's Law, which described the relationship between pressure and volume, as related to gases.

# Want to Learn More?

Chemistry is a constantly changing and expanding field of science. There are always new discoveries to be made. If you want to learn more about how chemistry works and how we use chemistry every day, examine some of these fantastic resources listed here.

## Chemistry Websites:

### BrainPop
www.brainpop.com/science/matterandchemistry/
Find answers to all your chemistry questions! This interactive site makes learning fun with the help of games, videos, and fascinating animations.

### Extreme Science
www.extremescience.com/zoom/index.php
Learn the science about some of the weirdest scientific phenomena on the planet.

### Science Made Simple
www.sciencemadesimple.com/
Get some great ideas for your next science project, and find fun chemistry activities you can do at home or with your friends and family.

### Strange Science
www.strangescience.net/
Learn more about the revolutionary scientists that were not always given their due during their lifetimes. All of these scientists' ideas changed the way we think about ourselves and our world.

### Try Science
www.tryscience.org/home.html
Learn trivia, find cool experiments to do at home, and watch live video of scientific projects on this kid-central website.

# Chemistry Books:

**Why Chemistry Matters** series. Crabtree Publishing, 2009.
This series uses common examples from everyday life to help explain basic chemistry.

**Chemistry,** by Dr. Bryson Gore. Stargazer Books, 2009. Learn all about acids and bases, as well as solutions, **enzymes**, and everyday chemical reactions. You will also learn more about the essential elements of life.

**Step into Science** series. Crabtree Publishing, 2010. Each book in this series explores a step in the scientific method.

**Matter**, by Rebecca Hunter. Raintree, 2001. This book explains what happens to atoms and molecules in various states of matter, and gives excellent examples of changes of state that happen in large-scale industries today.

**Chemistry**, by Dr. Ann Newmark. Dorling Kindersley, 2000. Learn about the first chemists, chemical reactions, noble gases, and other reactions such as **oxidation** and **reduction**. You can also learn more about the making of synthetic materials and the properties of metals.

# Places to Learn More:

## Chemical Heritage Foundation
### Philadelphia, Pennsylvania
The Chemical Heritage Foundation is an organization devoted to sharing the history of and importance of chemistry through exhibits, events, and education. Check out its website at: www.chemheritage.org

## National Museum of Natural History
### Washington, DC
One of the greatest museums in the world, visitors are free to explore many different exhibits of science, technology, and natural history in the various halls of this large museum complex.

## Staten Island Children's Museum
### Staten Island, New York
This interactive museum allows young visitors to get a close-up of the science behind living things, electricity, chemistry, and technology.

# Glossary

**acidic** Something that has the properties on an acid

**alchemy** An unscientific practice that attempted to transform matter into gold

**bacteria** Tiny life forms that can sometimes cause disease

**base** A compound that reacts with an acid to form a salt

**condense** To make something more dense or transform from a gas to a liquid

**corrode** To wear away gradually

**cosmetician** A person who applies cosmetics

**detergents** Any cleaning agent that, unlike soaps, are not prepared from fats or oils

**dispersion** To spread out

**enzymes** Proteins that originate from living cells

**fertilizers** A substance used to spark growth

**follicle** The sheath of cells and tissue that surround the root of a hair

**high blood pressure** A disease where the pressure of blood in the main arteries is abnormally high

**lubricated** When something has been made slippery or smooth to diminish friction

**nucleus** The central part of a cell about which other parts are gathered

**oxidation** The combination of a substance with oxygen

**particle** A tiny portion, piece, fragment, or amount

**reduction** The process or result of reducing or making less

**simulates** To create a likeness or model

**substances** Matter with uniform properties

**surfactant** Reduces the surface tension of a liquid, thus allowing it to penetrate solids

**synthetic** Something made from chemical synthesis, especially something that imitates a natural product

**theories** Ideas not yet proven

# Index